Blockchain Innovations

Shaping the Future of Finance and Technology

Table of Contents

Chapter 1. Introduction

Welcome to this Special Report: Blockchain Innovations - Shaping the Future of Finance and Technology. This comprehensive analysis seeks to demystify the complex yet intriguingly transformative technology – Blockchain. With blockchain's innovative roots impacting several key sectors, most notably finance and technology, the potential ahead is vast, yet can feel dauntingly technical. That's where this report strikes the perfect balance: delivering lucid, compelling explanations without sacrificing the depth of information, catering the needs of tech enthusiasts, novices, and all those keen to understand how blockchain might shift our worlds. It's your chance to delve into analyses from scholars, experts, and industry pioneers, unearthing how blockchain innovations are sculpting financial systems, digital processes, and the reality of a decentralized future. Its potential is powerful and transformative. Let this Special Report be your stepping stone to that future.

Chapter 2. Unraveling the Fundamentals of Blockchain

At the heart of blockchain technology lies digitized data, which forms the backbone of secure digital transactions. This amalgamation of information is only the tip of the iceberg when dissecting the complex and intriguing world of blockchain, a decentralized ledger.

2.1. The Anatomy of Blockchain

Blockchains are an interconnected web of blocks that store an array of transactional data. Each block contains a record of recent transactions, including transaction times and dates, participant details, and the transaction value.

The blockchain binds these blocks together through a unique identifier termed a 'hash'. Each block holds a unique hash and the hash of the previous block, creating a chain of these blocks connected chronologically. This sequential nature provides a timeline of transactions, which is highly transparent and traceable.

A blockchain once created preserves every transaction, rendering the alteration or deletion of past transactions near impossible. This immutability makes blockchain a highly secured way of transaction that is robust against fraudulent activities, which can be especially beneficial in industries such as banking, finance, supply chain management, and so on.

However, understanding the architecture of blockchain isn't about the confluence of data points but rather the convergence of three core principles: decentralization, transparency, and security.

2.2. The Principle of Decentralization

A centralized network has a single, primary authority that holds the power to oversee, control, and manipulate the transactions and data stored within the network. Meanwhile, decentralization means that the control of the network is distributed among all its users rather than centralized in one authority.

In a blockchain network, every user, or 'node', maintains a copy of the complete blockchain. When a new block is verified, it's added simultaneously to every node's version of the blockchain. This decentralized approach ensures the absence of a single point of failure and guarantees that the network remains functional even if some nodes become compromised or fail.

Demonstrating this power, Bitcoin, the pioneering digital currency, leverages blockchain to function without a central bank or single administrator. The decentralization principle forms the bedrock of all subsequent cryptocurrencies.

2.3. The Principle of Transparency

Transparency involves open access to information and data. With blockchain, every transaction is visible to all network participants, and every participant can view the entire transaction history.

However, it's relevant to note that blockchain's transparency doesn't contradict the privacy of its users. Despite the complete record of transactions on the blockchain being publicly visible, user identities are hidden via complex cryptography.

The transparency principle enhances blockchain's potential in areas including public auditing, supply chain management, and peer-to-peer transactions, where full visibility of transactions is required.

2.4. The Principle of Security

Blockchain boasts cryptographic security, which secures the stored information inside it. The hash function is a crucial part of this security facet.

Every block in a blockchain is intrinsically linked to its predecessor via its hash. Suppose an adversary alters one block's data; the hash of that block changes. This action disrupts the linkage with the next block in the chain, alerting the system of the discrepancy.

In addition to hashing, blockchain employs consensus algorithms to verify transactions. The most popular method is "Proof of Work," where validators (or 'miners') compete to solve complex computational problems. The first to solve the problem adds a block to the chain and receives a reward. This exhaustive process ensures a form of democratic transaction verification, further enhancing blockchain's overall security.

2.5. The Power of Smart Contracts

Smart contracts are self-executing contracts with the terms of the agreement between buyer and seller being directly written into lines of code. They hold the potential to automate routine, predictable transactions, thereby reducing the potential for disputes and strengthening contractual compliance.

A smart contract on the blockchain is a program that runs when predetermined conditions are met. It automatically validates a condition and then triggers a response. Since these smart contracts are autonomous, secure, and efficient, they can be used to exchange money, shares, property, or any valuable digital commodity.

The implementation of smart contracts in the blockchain landscape can broaden the scope of blockchain into numerous fields such as

insurance, real estate, healthcare, and even governmental systems
and public records.

2.6. Blockchains and Consensus Protocols

Blockchain networks require a consensus protocol to agree upon the
validity of transactions. It ensures every node maintains an identical
copy of the blockchain, thus creating a unified, tamper-resistant
system.

The most popular consensus protocol is the previously mentioned
Proof of Work (PoW). While PoW creates a highly secure network, it's
energy-intensive and slow. There is an alternative, less energy-
consuming protocol called Proof of Stake (PoS), where the validator's
chance of creating a block and the rewards they receive depend upon
the number of coins the validator holds.

Understanding the consensus protocols is important as they dictate
the speed, security, and environmental impact of blockchain
networks.

2.7. Conclusion

Unraveling the complex blockchain universe, we see a
revolutionizing technology shaping the future of financial and digital
systems. With its empowering decentralization, transparency, and
high level of security, blockchain paves the way for various
industries' future by overcoming traditional systems limitations.

Chapter 3. Exploring Blockchain's Evolution: From Bitcoin to DeFi

The story of blockchain begins in 2008 with a mysterious figure who went by the pseudonym Satoshi Nakamoto. In the aftermath of the 2008 financial crisis, Nakamoto released the Bitcoin whitepaper, laying the groundwork for the first blockchain. Nakamoto's conception of Bitcoin was not just a digital currency. Rather, it was a peer-to-peer digital cash system that did not rely on a central authority for control or oversight.

3.1. The Advent of Bitcoin

Understanding Bitcoin necessitates understanding blockchain. Each Bitcoin represents a transaction recorded on a public ledger known as the blockchain. The blockchain is a distributed, decentralized network that relies on a technique called cryptography to secure all transactions. Miners, or network participants, verify transactions by solving complex mathematical problems in a process known as mining, which adds new blocks to the chain.

Each block of the blockchain contains transaction data, a timestamp, and a reference (by a cryptographic hash) to the previous block, effectively linking all blocks together in a chain. The robustness of this technology lies in its resistance to manipulation. To edit one transaction, an ill-intentioned individual would need to alter not only the block including that transaction but all subsequent blocks - an improbable task given the computational power required.

Despite going live in January 2009, Bitcoin remained relatively obscure until 2017 when the price of Bitcoin skyrocketed, hitting nearly $20,000. The blockchain concept hit mainstream consciousness, attracting the attention of tech enthusiasts, investors, and financial institutions alike. Despite subsequent price corrections, the blockchain genie was out of the bottle, leading to a frenzy of exploration and experimentation in the technology and business sectors.

3.2. Etherum and Smart Contracts

In 2014, a new player sparked a significant evolution in blockchain technology. Launched by Vitalik Buterin, Ethereum was not merely a digital currency like Bitcoin; instead, it introduced smart contracts to the blockchain arena. Smart contracts are self-executing contracts with the terms of the agreement directly written into code. This means that when conditions in the contract are met, it will automatically execute the transaction.

Ethereum's smart contract capability transformed blockchain from a simple database for financial transactions into a platform with unlimited application potential. The Ethereum blockchain can store not only transactions but also programming logic, making it possible to create decentralized applications (DApps) hosted on the blockchain. Organizations started leveraging Ethereum to automate processes, create decentralized voting systems, implement supply chain tracking, and facilitate peer-to-peer rentals and sales, among other uses.

3.3. The Rise of DeFi

While Ethereum's introduction of Smart Contracts was transformative, a newer advancement called Decentralized Finance, or DeFi, has further pushed the envelope. Broadly speaking, DeFi refers to the use of blockchain and cryptocurrency to recreate and improve upon traditional financial systems. DeFi platforms operate without intermediaries such as banks, offering services like lending, borrowing, derivatives trading, payments, asset management and more.

DeFi runs on public blockchains (primarily Ethereum), meaning anyone can review, build on, or use them. This open accessibility and transparency upend traditional financial systems' most potent shortcomings, such as lack of access in underbanked regions, high transactional costs, slow processes, and institutional reliance.

Blockchain in the context of DeFi is not merely a technological tool—it is a foundational structural element, serving as the logistics backbone of a new, globally accessible decentralized economy. It's both liberating and powerful, and consistently highlights blockchain's potential as a universal standard for trustless systems.

But it's not entirely smooth sailing for DeFi. Some challenges exist, including smart contract bugs, scalability issues, and complex user experiences. However, ongoing innovations are addressing these roadblocks. Layer 2 solutions like Optimism and zkRollups promise to scale Ethereum, while successful DeFi interfaces such as Uniswap and Compound indicate a promising direction for user experiences.

3.4. Looking to the Future

As blockchain continues to permeate diverse sectors, it is becoming increasingly clear that Nakamoto's first digital currency, Bitcoin, was merely the tip of the iceberg. With smart contracts enabling blockchain's utility beyond cryptocurrencies and DeFi revolutionizing our approach towards financial systems, we're only beginning to explore the unprecedented potential of blockchain technology.

In the not-so-distant future, envision Internet of Things empowered by blockchain for enhanced security, proof-of-stake replacing energy-extensive proof-of-work, interoperable cross-chain protocols becoming commonplace, governance systems transforming under the influence of Decentralized Autonomous Organizations, to mention a few.

Sealing this chapter, remember: Blockchain is not an elusive science project. It's a technological breakthrough akin to the emergence of the internet itself. Where we go from here requires concerted efforts from technology leaders, regulatory bodies, and every individual keen on embracing this decentralization paradigm. While the journey ahead can seem technical and daunting, it is pivotal in constructing our future – a transparent, efficient, and disruptive future. In this era where data privacy, transparency, and freedom hold immense significance, these decentralized innovations are not just shaping the financial and technological landscapes but also reinventing human interactions and systems at an unprecedented scale. Welcome to the age of decentralization.

Chapter 4. Decentralized Finance (DeFi): A New Era for Finance

In the last few years, there has been a seismic shift in the world of finance. A new era, often called Decentralized Finance (DeFi), has emerged, born from the digital realm and powered by cutting-edge technologies like cryptocurrency, smart contracts, and, most importantly, blockchain.

This revolution is not just a facelift of traditional finance but represents a profound reimagining. DeFi seeks a robust, open financial system without gates and gatekeepers, eliminating the need for intermediaries while maximizing accessibility to a spectrum of financial products and services.

4.1. The Core Concept of Decentralized Finance (DeFi)

Decentralized finance, or "DeFi," is a term that encapsulates a variety of financial applications and operations in cryptocurrency or blockchain geared toward obliterating financial intermediaries. DeFi brings to the table the ethos of decentralization by leveraging smart contracts built on Ethereum, the world's second-largest cryptocurrency platform.

Smart contracts are self-executing contracts embedded with the terms of an agreement directly written into lines of code. They offer vast possibilities to automate various aspects of financial transactions, delivering transactions and interaction with reduced (sometimes vanished) need for human intervention.

The DeFi movement aims to promote a global, open alternative to every existing financial service, such as savings, loans, insurance, trading, and more. This open basic infrastructure, composed of decentralized networks, allows anyone in the world with an internet-connected device to access these financial services.

4.2. The Expanding Universe of DeFi

The range and sophistication of DeFi applications have seen explosive growth. For the uninitiated, a leap into this dynamic world can seem overwhelming due to the wealth of terminology, each describing an often uniquely innovative financial product or service.

Let's examine some of the critical terms and concepts:

- Dapps (Decentralized applications): Autonomous smart contract-driven applications that run on a blockchain network.

- Stablecoins: Cryptocurrencies pegged to the value of more stable assets such as gold or USD.

- Yield Farming: Users earning rewards for staking their tokens in a DeFi protocol to earn more tokens.

- Liquidity Pools: Pooled funds that provide liquidity through smart contracts to users in a DeFi market.

- AMMs (Automated Market Makers): Algorithms that set the price of tokens in decentralized exchange markets.

This rich array of DeFi applications already mirrors an entire ecosystem of traditional banking services, yet delivered without a bank's hierarchical structure.

4.3. Advantages of DeFi

One major draw of DeFi applications is their potential to supply financial services to people who, until now, were unbanked or underbanked. Traditional banking systems have often failed to reach all corners of the globe, but DeFi can potentially offer a solution to this age-old problem.

As long as someone has an internet connection and a digital wallet, they can access a wide range of DeFi applications and services, often with no need to undertake complicated identification procedures.

Another advantage is the ability to yield high returns. By lending out their cryptocurrencies, users can earn lucrative yields over a period. With the global interest rates at historic lows, and in some places even below zero, this has become an attractive option for many.

Furthermore, the transparency that blockchain technology provides is another essential factor for DeFi. Each transaction is publicly recorded on the blockchain allowing for an unprecedented level of auditability.

4.4. Challenges and Risks with DeFi

While offering a promising and indeed revolutionary vision of the future financial systems, DeFi isn't without its challenges and risks. Not least of these is the complexity of the technology. For many, the concepts behind blockchain and cryptocurrency are tough to understand. This complexity poses a barrier to mass adoption.

Moreover, the regulatory environment is, at best, murky. Most governments around the world are yet to figure out how to categorize, let alone regulate or tax cryptocurrencies. This uncertainty can be a significant risk for those investing in DeFi.

The lack of a central governing body means the responsibility for security falls largely onto the individual. In case of loss or theft, there is often no recourse to retrieve stolen assets.

Another considerable risk is highly volatile cryptocurrencies, which can lead to similarly volatile returns on DeFi applications.

4.5. Future Potential of DeFi

In its current form, DeFi is already upending the world of finance. Despite its challenges, the potential it bears is too high to be ignored. It's not just that DeFi offers a world where anyone with a digital wallet can access financial services; It's also creating a future where these services are entirely customizable, as Dapps can be built atop each other and functions combined to meet users' specific needs.

Through innovation, education, and regulatory advances, DeFi has the potential to become a mainstream staple of the financial world. It could signal not only a new era for finance but the next stage in financial democracy. However, the path to this future, while illuminated with promise, remains fraught with challenges that must be navigated with caution, understanding, and collaborative effort.

Indeed, the DeFi wave has only just begun, promising to reshape the horizon of finance globally in ways previously unimaginable. As this foundation expands and diversifies, it will unlock more opportunities for innovation, penetrating deeper into the financial space, and further democratizing finance's vast, complex world.

Chapter 5. Blockchain in Fintech: A Paradigm Shift

The advent of blockchain technology has unlocked a new era in the financial industry referred to as Fintech (Financial technology). It presents an array of potentially transformative possibilities for participants across the financial spectrum - from banks to insurers, from government bodies to everyday consumers. The transfiguration thrown open by blockchain in Fintech is pivotal, forceful, and here to stay.

5.1. The Current Financial System's Limitations and the Need for Blockchain

The traditional financial system has long been perceived as a highly centralized mechanism in which a small number of entities maintain authority. This structure has inherent limitations. It not only slows down transaction processes but also reduces the system's transparency and raises security concerns. Additionally, the intermediaries involved increase the transaction costs and make cross border transactions complex and inefficient.

This is where blockchain technology steps in. It challenges these orthodox structures by eliminating the need for intermediarity, creating a more transparent, secure, and efficient system. Blockchain's decentralized nature allows direct transactions between parties, making financial processes more streamlined and agile.

5.2. Conceptualizing Blockchain Technology: An Overview

Born out of the innovations underpinning Bitcoin, the original blockchain presented a public ledger system which kept a permanent and immutable record of all transactions. This foundational technology provides a way to confirm transactions, manage digital assets, and record data securely without the need for a central authority or intermediary.

At its rudimentary core, blockchain represents a distributed, digital ledger where recorded transactions are stored in a block and linked to each other via cryptographic principles. Once entered, data cannot be tampered or altered. This feature engenders security, mitigates fraud, and reinforces trust among parties - highly valuable qualities in the financial sector.

As a basic model, blockchain's concept comprises three essential components:

1. Blocks, which register and store transaction data

2. Mining, a process of validating and adding transaction records to the blockchain

3. Consensus algorithm, a protocol to prevent double-spending and to maintain integrity and harmony in the system

5.3. Implications of Blockchain for Fintech

Blockchain technology can dramatically repaint the Fintech landscape in several profound ways.

1. Lower Transaction Costs:

By eliminating intermediaries, blockchain can significantly reduce transaction fees. Banks and other financial institutions often impose charges for the services they provide. Due to its peer-to-peer transaction mechanism, blockchain can slash these costs, driving economic efficiency.

1. Heightened Security and Fraud Reduction:

Blockchain's immutable ledger provides an iron-clad layer of security. It prevents deceitful activities and cyber threats because, once recorded, the data cannot be retroactively changed without altering all subsequent blocks, a task near impossible.

1. Improved Process Efficiency:

Blockchain's transparent nature helps fast-track verification processes, optimizes operational procedures, and significantly cuts down on errors and disputes.

1. Greater Accessibility:

Blockchain can democratize financial services by enabling access to unbanked or underbanked populations worldwide. Through digital identity verification and secure peer-to-peer transactions, blockchain can extend financial services to people who have been historically marginalized.

5.4. Blockchain Use Cases in Fintech

Blockchain's potential in Fintech is vast. Here is a snapshot of some use cases that are transforming the Fintech domain:

1. Decentralized Finance (DeFi): These platforms aim to replace traditional financial intermediaries with peer-to-peer networks. Examples include decentralized borrowing and lending platforms, insurance providers, and asset management tools.

2. Cryptocurrencies: These leveraged blockchain's innate capacities to perform financial functions in a decentralized, digital manner. Bitcoin and Ethereum are two notable examples.

3. Smart Contracts: These are self-executing contracts where terms and conditions are written in code. They eliminate the need for intermediaries, thus reducing costs, and can be used in various applications like mortgage loans, insurance claims, and securities trading.

4. Digital Identity: By providing a transparent, immutable record that can automatically verify identities, blockchain addresses security concerns of digital identity in the financial sector.

5. Cross-Border Payments: Blockchain drastically reduces the time and cost involved in cross-border transactions, making them efficient and transparent.

5.5. Challenges and the Way Forward

For all its promise, blockchain technology is not without its hurdles. The lack of clear regulatory frameworks, scalability issues, and public perception are among the key challenges. However, as technology and understanding evolve, these obstacles may diminish over time. In fact, the current trajectory and studies suggest a disruptive yet prosperous future where blockchain could represent the backbone of the Fintech industry.

Despite these potential barriers, the blockchain's role in revolutionizing the Fintech landscape is undeniable. From reimagining payments to enhancing digital identity, blockchain has been steadily disrupting traditional financial mechanisms. As organizations catapult into the world of blockchain, it begets the reimagination of financial technology, setting a new paradigm that likely signifies the future of financial services worldwide. Through this transformation, blockchain delivers a lens to a future marked by decentralization, seamlessness, and crucially, democratization of financial access.

Chapter 6. Digital Identity and Security in the Blockchain Era

The socio-economic landscape of the world is shifting, bringing digital identity and security to the forefront of the conversation. Due to the integration of technology in various aspects of our lives, managing digital identity has become a critical concern. Traditionally, each organization where you share your information, such as a bank, maintains its separate database. However, with each additional digital account, multiplying the risk of identity theft and fraud. Enter blockchain – a potential remedy to these woes.

6.1. Understanding Digital Identity

A digital identity is a collection of electronically stored attributes and credentials that are used for online transactions. It includes numerous digital footprints, such as social security numbers, bank account details, email addresses, etc. With the advent of the internet, the importance of digital identities has grown multi-fold, enabling services like online shopping, banking, and social networking. However, unfortunately, identity theft has also proliferically grown. In 2020 alone, about 1.4 billion records were exposed in data breaches, many containing sensitive identity information.

6.2. Blockchain Enhancing Digital Identity Security

Blockchain technology acts as a public ledger, maintaining an immutable and transparent record of all transactions. Each participating node in the network holds a copy of the entire blockchain, making tampering or altering a record nearly impossible. Blockchain's decentralized model for storing data inherently bolsters the security of digital identities.

To understand this, consider a standard model of digital identity storage, where a centralized authority stores all user data. This model creates a "single point of failure," where if the central authority is compromised, all user data is compromised. However, in a blockchain model, the user data is systematically spread across a network of nodes, eliminating that single point of failure and increasing the resilience of the system.

6.3. Self-Sovereign Identity (SSI) and Blockchain

Blockchain aids in the advent of Self-Sovereign Identity (SSI), where individuals or organizations have sole ownership over their digital identities, controlling how, when, and to whom their identity data is shared. If implemented, SSI can uproot the current digital identity landscape by providing a secure, transparent, user-centric model for managing identities.

Blockchain-based digital identities can offer a high level of security and control to the users, with the following advantages:

1. Sovereignty: Users have full control over their personal data.

2. Trust: Blockchain being a decentralized and transparent system helps build trust among users.

3. Access: It enables global access to financial services even for unbanked populations.

4. Security: Blockchain reduces the risk of identity theft, fraud, and privacy breaches.

5. Interoperability: It allows safe and secure sharing of data across

platforms.

6.4. Risks and Challenges in Implementing Blockchain for Digital Identity

While the potential of blockchain in managing digital identity is immense, it does come with its own set of challenges and risks. First and foremost, blockchain is not inherently privacy-preserving. While it can provide transparency and integrity, ensuring private data stays private is still a challenge today. There is also the risk of private keys being stolen or lost, resulting in irreversible loss of data.

Another major challenge is the question of jurisdiction and governance. Since blockchain networks are borderless, determining jurisdiction in case of a conflict or dispute can be difficult. The adoption of blockchain technology for digital identity will require the establishment of robust legal and regulatory frameworks to protect users.

Additionally, blockchain's complex technical nature could be a barrier to adoption for the masses. It requires a good deal of technical know-how, something that may take time and significant educational efforts.

6.5. Conclusion

As technology continues to evolve, so too does the importance of digital identity and security. Blockchain technology could radically change how we manage digital identities, providing a secure, transparent, and efficient solution. However, the technology is still relatively new and has its challenges. It requires careful planning, robust legislation, and the adoption of best practices to truly realize its full potential.

While the road to blockchain-powered digital identity may be fraught with challenges, it holds the promise of a more secure, private, and user-centric identity management system. It's an intriguing opportunity, one that could bring us closer to a truly digital and decentralized future.

This marks the end of our journey into the depths of Digital Identity and Security in the Blockchain era. However, remember, this is just the tip of the iceberg. Consider it a stepping stone, an initiation into a wider world of knowledge, ready to be explored.

Chapter 7. Smart Contracts: The Building Blocks of Blockchain Applications

Upon entering the engaging realm of blockchain applications, one cannot overlook the linchpin enabling this infamous revolution – Smart Contracts. These self-executing contracts with the terms of the agreement directly written into lines of code have become the cornerstone for the countless applications blockchain technology offers.

7.1. Overview

Smart contracts were first proposed by Nick Szabo, an American computer scientist and cryptographer, long before the inception of blockchain technology. Defined by Szabo in 1994, these contracts were designed to facilitate, verify, or enforce the negotiation or performance of a contract using cryptographic protocols.

It was not until the arrival of blockchain technology, a digital, decentralized ledger that records transactions across many computers in such a way that the registered transactions cannot be altered retroactively, that smart contracts truly came into their own. A clear illustration of this leap forward can be witnessed through the expansive ecosystem built around the Ethereum blockchain.

The Ethereum platform, launched in 2015, has distinguished itself by enabling developers to run smart contracts on its blockchain. It provided a solid foundation to usher in a surge of new applications, all made possible by these programmable contracts.

7.2. Smart Contract Basics

Smart contracts function by leveraging pre-set digital rules. These rules outline what actions will be undertaken when specific conditions have been met. For example, in a car insurance agreement, if the car suffers damage related to an accident, a smart contract will automatically activate the payment to the insured party.

Rather than relying on intermediaries such as banks or lawyers, smart contracts execute agreements in an automated, transparent, secure, and trustworthy mode. They act as a digital facilitator, enabling participants to engage in financial transactions, exchange of digital assets, or even the execution of complex multi-party protocols.

7.3. Programming of Smart Contracts

Smart contracts are constructed using blockchain-specific programming languages, such as Solidity for Ethereum-based contracts. The contracts are written in such a way that they are inviolable – they're designed to ensure that no single party can modify the terms once they are established and activated. This fosters transparency and trust among the participants involved.

The written agreement is then placed on the blockchain, where a specific code, or hash, is created for it. This hash enables the identification and tracking of this asset on the blockchain, ensuring its security and immutability.

7.4. The Role of Smart Contracts in Blockchain Applications

Smart contracts serve as the foundation for decentralized

applications, or DApps. These applications run on a peer-to-peer network of computers rather than a single computer. They serve a vast range of functions from executing simple transactions to managing complex operations in sectors like supply chain, healthcare, real estate, and finance, among others.

In finance, smart contracts have been pivotal in the creation of Decentralized Finance (DeFi) applications, which aim to revolutionize financial transactions by eliminating the need for intermediaries. Similarly, in the supply chain domain, they help increase transparency and efficiency by automating the traceability and authentication of products.

7.5. Advantages of Smart Contracts

Moreover, smart contracts offer several advantages over traditional contract systems. To start with, they cut down the need for intermediaries, reducing costs and increasing efficiency. The contracts also ensure a high level of security, as once a contract is stored on a blockchain, it is protected by the same high-level cryptographic techniques that secure cryptocurrencies.

Another advantage lies in their automation, which means the contract self-executes once the conditions in its clause are fulfilled, leaving no room for delays or human error. On top of that, smart contracts offer the potential for real-time auditing, enhancing the transparency and traceability of transactions.

7.6. Legal and Regulatory Challenges of Smart Contracts

Despite these benefits, the application of smart contracts also invites legal and regulatory dilemmas. The question of legality is often raised, given the automation and self-execution feature of smart contracts. If conflicts arise out of a transaction, it becomes challenging to identify a recourse mechanism. Furthermore, the cross-border nature of blockchain transactions can also lead to jurisdictional complexities.

Moreover, most jurisdictions lack specific regulations addressing smart contracts, creating potential uncertainties around their enforceability and the responsibilities of the involved parties.

7.7. Looking Ahead: The Future of Smart Contracts

The future of smart contracts looks promising despite these challenges. As blockchain technology matures, we can expect smart contracts to become more sophisticated and versatile, expanding their applications across varied sectors. Integration with other emerging tech, like artificial intelligence and the Internet of Things, will only add to their potential, paving the way for a truly automated and decentralized future.

Smart Contracts have indeed become the building blocks of blockchain applications, streamlining processes, cutting costs, and bolstering trust among parties. Whether you are a tech enthusiast or a novice trying to understand the blockchain world, a deep dive into smart contracts offers an insightful sneak peek into how our financial and technological systems are poised for a decisive leap.

Chapter 8. Unleashing the Potential of Decentralized Autonomous Organizations (DAOs)

Decentralized Autonomous Organizations, commonly known as DAOs, are the harbingers of a new decentralized era of governance and economic interaction. These digital entities, powered by blockchain technology, are self-governing, operate without intermediaries and enable individuals to collaborate in a democratized system.

8.1. Emergence of Decentralized Autonomous Organizations

The systemic inadequacies of traditional organizations gave rise to a decentralized alternative – DAOs. The creation of DAOs is essentially the manifestation of blockchain's potential for transparency, security, and decentralization.

The idea behind DAOs was introduced by the members of the cryptocurrency community amidst the growing influence of blockchain in 2013. The essence was simple: to set up an organization in which (1) decisions were automated, (2) contracts were upheld by computer code, and (3) operating systems were decentralized. Thus, the DAO was born — a revolutionary concept that had the potential to reshape economies and realign power structures.

8.2. How Do DAOs Work?

A DAO operates using smart contracts, computer programs that automatically execute the terms of an agreement upon fulfillment of certain conditions. These smart contracts provide a trustworthy, non-manipulatable framework for the interactions within the DAO.

Participants in a DAO interact with these smart contracts by putting forward proposals or voting on existing ones. These proposals can range from changes in the organization's rules to allocation of funds for specific projects. Any changes to the DAO are approved only when a majority consensus is reached among the participants.

DAOs also leverage tokens to facilitate operations and allow participants to voice their opinions. Tokens are usually procured through an initial buy-in, or 'Initial Coin Offering' (ICO), facilitating a decentralized distribution of tokens at the organization's inception.

8.3. DAOs: Advantages and Potential

The potential of DAOs is vast and transformative. They offer several advantages over traditional organizations:

1. **Decentralization**: DAOs remove the need for central controlling authorities, promoting a system of collaboratively shared power.

2. **Transparency**: All decisions are open for scrutiny by any participant ensuring transparency and accountability.

3. **Automation**: By leveraging smart contracts, DAOs automate decision-making and execution processes, eliminating the need for middlemen.

4. **Security**: Blockchain's inherent — and therefore DAO's — security makes them highly resistant to fraud and manipulation.

5. **Inclusivity**: DAOs ensure every participant's voice is heard,

promoting a democratic decision-making process.

8.4. Understanding the Challenges

While DAOs promise a revolution, they are susceptible to a range of challenges. Understanding these can help us better navigate the roadblocks to truly leveraging their potential.

DAOs are still relatively new and face legal and regulatory uncertainties. Moreover, its always-online and immutable nature leads to exposure to potential tacit security threats that may exploit coding vulnerabilities. Similarly, consensus formation which is one of the pillars of DAOs, may also become an issue, especially in large groups with diverging interests.

Despite these challenges, the potential of DAOs transcends the obstacles they face. By considering these drawbacks and developing protective remedies, DAOs can harness their full potential and reshape the landscape of governance and economic interaction.

8.5. Case Studies

Delving into some real-life examples can provide a vivid and tangible understanding of DAOs' functions and impacts.

The DAO, established in 2016, was one of the first attempts at creating a DAO. Despite it succumbing to a hack, it established many principles DAOs follow today.

Another notable DAO is **MakerDAO**, which oversees the stablecoin DAI. Operating since 2015, it allows its users to participate in governance decisions about DAI's stability mechanism using its governance token, MKR.

8.6. Conclusion

DAOs, with their revolutionary structure, have the potential to disrupt existing forms of organization. By leveraging blockchain technology's intrinsic traits of decentralization, transparency, and security, they open up a myriad of possibilities in various sectors.

While DAOs face certain challenges, the potential advantages provide ample motivation for continuing innovation and experimentation in this field. The steady proliferation of DAOs across various sectors is a testament to their potential and long-term viability.

Ultimately, the evolution and growth of DAOs represent a shift towards a more inclusive, transparent, and decentralized future. The blockchain-enabled democratization of organizations is poised to revolutionize our societal and economic structures, aiding in humanity's march towards a more decentralized world.

Chapter 9. The Impact of Blockchain on Supply Chain and IoT

Blockchain technology, with its inherent qualities of transparency, security, and immutability, has far-reaching ramifications for numerous industry sectors, including Supply Chain Management (SCM) and the Internet of Things (IoT). Its potential in these areas, while currently exploited to varying degrees, points toward an exciting era of transformation and efficiency.

9.1. The Blockchain Revolution in Supply Chain Management

Supply chain, by definition, involves a network of interconnected businesses responsible for the production and distribution of a specific product or service. This network is often riddled with inefficiencies due to opaque operations, fraudulent activities, and redundant intermediaries. Blockchain presents itself as a potential panacea to these issues.

One of the foremost benefits of blockchain in SCM is the introduction of an immutable and transparent ledger. Every step of a product's journey, from production to the end-user, can be logged on the blockchain. This information, once written, can neither be forged nor altered, ensuring enhanced security and reliability in tracking goods.

Imagine a scenario where a consumer wants to verify the authenticity and origin of a product they purchased. With a blockchain-enabled supply chain, they would have a clear path of information, starting from the raw material, to the production process, all through to the final delivery. Thus, it is not only transparency and security that is increased, but also consumer trust and confidence.

Further enhancing trust and efficiency, blockchain can also minimize intermediaries. By utilizing smart contracts - autonomous digital contracts that execute when specified conditions are met - transparency can be ensured in every business transaction removing the need for trust intermediaries.

9.2. Transforming IoT with Blockchain

The Internet of Things (IoT) represents a vast network of connected devices that collect and share data. As the number of IoT devices continues to explode, management and security concerns rise in tandem. Blockchain, by virtue of its decentralized, secure, and transparent nature, offers solutions to these pivotal issues.

Blockchain can create an immutable, tamper-proof record of all the messages exchanged between IoT devices. This feature enhances the security of IoT communications drastically, helping mitigate risks associated with data tampering or fabrication.

In addition, blockchain's decentralized operation disintermediates the need for central data hubs. Instead, each IoT device becomes part of a distributed network, safely storing and sharing data. This structure significantly reduces the vulnerabilities associated with centralized storage systems, thereby preventing single-point failures.

IoT devices can also leverage smart contracts for automation and efficiency. An example of this might be intelligent thermostats that automatically initiate energy purchase when the household's energy levels drop below a certain level, leading to more efficient power utilization and reduced human intervention.

9.3. Global Case Studies on SCM and IoT

Various companies across the globe are already harnessing the potential of blockchain in SCM and IoT. For instance, IBM and Maersk spearheaded a blockchain platform called TradeLens to digitize and streamline global shipping operations. TradeLens reported in 2020 that it was processing 10 million shipments a month, with a growing list of participants such as customs authorities, freight forwarders, and port operators.

Walmart is another prime example that employed blockchain to trace the source of food products. The transparency offered by blockchain technology helped reduce contamination risks and bolster customer confidence as they could track their produce from the farm to their table.

On the IoT front, IOTA provides an illustrative example. The non-profit foundation developed a secure, feeless, "blockless" distributed ledger that supports data transfer between IoT devices. With no mining and scalability restrictions, this novel "tangle" architecture marks a significant step ahead in the IoT-blockchain integration.

9.4. The Way Forward

The innovative intersections of blockchain with SCM and IoT present a transformative future rife with possibilities. The implementation is in nascent stages, and challenges such as regulatory constraints, interoperability, and transition complexities persist. But the paradigm shift is inevitable. The potential cost savings, improved efficiency, enhanced security, and consumer trust that blockchain promises are too compelling to ignore.

In these early stages of adaptation and exploration, it becomes crucial to foster blockchain literacy, implement suitable legal frameworks, encourage industry cooperation, and support research and development. As we move forward, the evolving landscape of SCM and IoT through blockchain technology will undoubtedly redefine business processes, consumer experiences, and the global digital infrastructure itself.

Chapter 10. Predictive Analysis: Future Trends in Blockchain Technology

To predict the future trends of blockchain technology, it's crucial to understand not only where we are now, but how we got here. Blockchain sprouted from the digital soil of technology and finance, but it is quickly proving capable of growing beyond these confines, shooting tendrils of transformative potential into a fascinating diversity of sectors and industries.

10.1. Evolution as Foundation

The first blockchain was conceptualized by a person (or group of people) using the pseudonym Satoshi Nakamoto in 2008, showing us a groundbreaking way forward in the world of digital transactions. This technology became an integral part of Bitcoin, acting as the public ledger for all transactions on its network. Since then, its application was realized to transcend beyond cryptocurrency, birthing the era of blockchain 2.0, which included Ethereum, Ripple, and others.

10.2. The Business Blockchain Boom

While technology startups and cryptocurrency enthusiasts were among the first to experiment with the blockchain, the last few years have seen a marked shift. Large, traditional businesses are stepping into the fold. Major corporations such as IBM, Amazon, and Microsoft, to mention a few, have seen the latent potential of blockchain technology and have started investing their resources in developing it for diverse applications. This has bolstered the market requirements for decentralization and transparency in businesses.

10.3. Interoperable Blockchains: A Network of Networks

One of the underlying trends in the blockchain ecosystem is the pursuit of interoperability. It means facilitating seamless communication between diverse blockchains, much akin to a kind of blockchain internet or a "network of networks". This would provide an immense boost to the development and functionality of decentralized applications (dApps), creating an integrated ecosystem of blockchain solutions. Interoperability will not only stimulate blockchain industrialization but will also actively support cross-blockchain transactions.

10.4. The Confluence of AI and Blockchain

Another clear trend is the fusion between AI (Artificial Intelligence) and blockchain. Both these technologies are at the forefront of digital transformation, and their integration can prove to be a powerful combination. While AI focuses on making machines mimic human intelligence, blockchain provides a tamper-proof, transparent, and decentralized database.

Pairing these two technologies brings ample opportunities. Planned on-chain AI decisions could deal impeccably with privacy issues, data monopoly concerns, and in ensuring the equitable distribution of AI's benefits. Meanwhile, blockchain could address AI's trust issues, provide transparency on AI decisions, and ensure the data used for AI is reliable.

10.5. Token Economy: The Age of Digital Assets

The idea of a token economy is fundamentally tied to the concept of blockchain. Here, tokens, recorded on a blockchain, can represent a vast array of tangible and intangible assets. As blockchain evolves, we are seeing a growing emphasis on the token economy. From tokenized real estate and intellectual property to decentralized finance (DeFi) and non-fungible tokens (NFTs), the opportunities are vast.

10.6. Smart Contracts: Powering the Decentralized Future

An integral part of the blockchain 2.0 evolution, smart contracts, self-executing contracts with the terms of agreement directly embedded into code lines, are poised to revolutionize traditional contract law and reduce red tape. As a result, they have the potential to transform industries including, but not limited to, real estate, law, banking, healthcare, and government.

10.7. Blockchain and Data Privacy

As the world becomes increasingly digital, data privacy becomes a growing concern. Given its fundamental design, blockchain offers an ideal solution. Its decentralized nature turns traditional data handling on its head, gives users control over their personal information, and makes it more secure against hacking attempts.

10.8. Conclusion

From these future trends, what emerges is a picture of a world that, while technocentric, is paradoxically more human. Leveraging blockchain's capabilities points towards a future with greater transparency, decentralization, privacy, and equity. Blockchain's potential for change is as extensive as it is exciting. From transforming financial systems to protecting people's privacy in an increasingly digital world, blockchain technology can become the backbone of a future that is emerging right before our eyes. The trends we've explored here are just the beginning, and it is up to us to embrace and develop the potential that blockchain technology undeniably holds.

Chapter 11. Real-world Case Studies: Successful Blockchain Implementations

The versatility of blockchain technology is best demonstrated through its real-world applications. Cutting-edge blockchain implementations across multiple industries have revolutionized traditional processes, bolstering efficiency, security, and transparency. In this chapter, we delve into various successful blockchain use cases that are trailblazers of this technological revolution.

11.1. Case 1: De Beers and Everledger—Pioneering Blockchain in the Diamond Industry

De Beers, the international corporation with a stronghold on the diamond mining industry, adopted blockchain technology with their innovative platform, Tracr. This platform utilizes blockchain to track the journey of a diamond, from the mine to the customer. Thus, it ensures the provenance of diamonds, flagging artificially enhanced or conflict stones, and enhancing customer trust.

In a similar vein, Everledger utilizes blockchain to create secure, immutable digital versions of real-world diamonds and high-value items. Launched in 2015, Everledger has, to date, captured the unique attributes of over 1.6 million diamonds on the blockchain, ensuring traceability and discouraging the trade of conflict diamonds and counterfeit gems.

11.2. Case 2: IBM Food Trust—Securing the Supply Chain

IBM Food Trust, a collaborative network of growers, processors, wholesalers, distributors, manufacturers, and retailers, has made strides in enhancing visibility and accountability across the food supply chain. Leveraging IBM Blockchain technology, the Food Trust provides end-to-end traceability, drastically reducing the time needed to trace a food item from store to farm.

During a contamination incident in 2018, Walmart could trace a pack of sliced mangos to its original farm using this system in 2.2 seconds, a process that previously took almost seven days. This innovation ensures the safety of food products consumed and combats fraudulent practices in the industry.

11.3. Case 3: Estonia—Implementing National e-Governance

Estonia became the first country to integrate blockchain on a national level. The country's tech-driven government introduced e-governance services, such as e-residency, i-voting, e-health, and e-Tax, all utilizing blockchain. Known as X-road, this platform links together various public and private sector e-service databases, providing unprecedented levels of security and transparency in public service delivery.

11.4. Case 4: Maersk and IBM—Creating TradeLens for Global trade

Maersk, the world's largest shipping company, partnered with IBM to create TradeLens, a blockchain-enabled shipping solution aimed at promoting more efficient and secure global trade. Shipping container information, customs documents, and bills of lading are all stored in the blockchain, providing an immutable audit trail.

As an immutable, distributed, and tamper-resistant ledger, TradeLens gives each participant in the supply chain complete visibility into the container's journey. As a result, delays and disputes are drastically reduced, fostering trust and boosting efficiency.

11.5. Case 5: Royal Bank of Canada (RBC)—Streamlining Payments

The Royal Bank of Canada utilized blockchain to automate credit scores and verify the identities of new clients. In a practical application, RBC leveraged a decentralized identity platform to ease the process of opening up new bank accounts. The traditional weeks-long verification process was reduced to mere minutes.

This application serves as a clear indication of how blockchain technology can significantly ramp up efficiency in financial institutions while ensuring security and eliminating the attendant identity fraud cases often associated with such transactions.

11.6. Case 6: Axoni and DTCC—Transforming Capital Markets

The Depository Trust & Clearing Corporation (DTCC), in collaboration with fintech company Axoni, launched a blockchain platform poised to transform post-trade lifecycle events of credit derivatives. By removing the need for manual reconciliation and automating confirmation procedures, the blockchain-based platform ensures real-time, transparent updates for everyone in the trade network—enhancing efficiency, security, and cost-effectiveness.

Each of these examples demonstrates the multidimensional potential of blockchain technology. What they have in common, despite spanning various sectors, is their success in harnessing blockchain's capacity for providing security, transparency, and process optimization. Although still emerging, the transformative power of blockchain is undeniable. These successful implementations herald a future where blockchain technology becomes a cornerstone of global infrastructures, driving innovation and remaking long-standing systems and processes.

www.ingramcontent.com/pod-product-compliance
Lightning Source LLC
Chambersburg PA
CBHW071008260726
48661CB00007B/2845